The Silver Cord

Also by Brenda Eldridge and published by Ginninderra Press

Poetry
The Silver Cord
It's All Good
A Personal View
Facing Cancer
From My Garden
Best Heard & Seen
Scarves
Tangled Roots: new & selected poems
Elemental (Pocket Poets)
Forgotten Dreams (Pocket Poets)

Non-fiction
Down by the River
Tales From My Patagonia
It's Still Out There
There's a Rainbow Serpent In My Garden
Eastwards
From Patagonia to Australia
Forty Green (Pocket Places)

Edited by Brenda Eldridge and published by Ginninderra Press
Brave Enough To Be a Poet
The Heart of Port Adelaide
Collecting Writers

Brenda Eldridge

The Silver Cord

The Silver Cord
ISBN 978 1 74027 538 5
Copyright © text Brenda Eldridge 2009
Cover photo: Annette Jolly

First published 2009 by
GINNINDERRA PRESS
PO Box 3461 Port Adelaide SA 5015
www.ginninderrapress.com.au

Contents

Life – a Gift	7
5th April 1991 – A Day To Be Reckoned With	8
Finding the Way Back	9
White Sail	11
Earthly Silk	12
Grapes	13
Shimmering Diamond	14
Cockatoos	15
Liquid Glass	16
Enchanted	17
Tranquillity	19
Dawning	20
Fragment In Time	21
Uncontained Joy	22
Defiance	23
At the End of the Day	24
Parading Down the Parade	25
Cheeky	26
Paradise Interchange	27
Annette	28
A Lament	29
Music In the Park	30
Hard Road	31
Unless You Are Brave	33
Living and Knowing	34
Dreaming In the Sand	35
Discovery	36
Veterans	38
The Eleventh Hour	40
Laughter	42
Taming the Wild	44
Restoration	45

Watery Mind	47
Grieve No More	48
Sunday-afternoon Amazon	49
Dreams	50
Seduction	51
Stirring Passions	52
Dying Brightness	53
Innocence	54
Sticky Little Hands	56
Published	58
Those In the Sea	59
Pause For a Moment	61
Evening	62
Smoke Gets In Your Eyes	63
A Moment of Grace	64
Home To the Sun	65
Lovely Surprise	66
Debarking	67
Icelandic Poppies	68
Homeward Bound	69
Pilgrimage	71
Tapestry of Sound	72
Go To Hell	73
Gone Forever	74
It's All Right, Mark	75
Silver Cord	76
Afterword	77

Life – a Gift

Life, relentlessly you pull and tug
And once, like a mindless marionette, I danced.
Blissfully unaware of the magnificence of your gift
Carelessly drifting securely through childhood
Encapsulated, nurtured endlessly by my parents' devotion.

I flaunted you with the blithe arrogance of youth
Surrendering in unresisting, gay abandon, as you beckoned,
Blindly denying the existence of cruelty
Till you savaged my soul with uncompromising brutality
And I must lay my son in the embrace of the earth

Driven by despair, I wanted to leave you too
Yet in the eyes of my beloved you shone pure
Unable to go, I fought to want to stay with you
Your bounty was spread all about me
A splendid, panoramic wonder

I discovered your constancy everywhere
I didn't know till then you and loving were the same
An inherent sense of joy makes me laugh deliciously
Others are overcome by the urge to join in
In unity we dispel the gloom

5th April 1991 – A Day To Be Reckoned With

Voice on the telephone, 'Are the police there yet'
Brenda, 'Where's Mark?'
Another voice, 'Mark's dead. He shot himself in the shop
   this afternoon.'

Three months later

The pall of death is black they say, the colour of despair,
But mine has threads of gleaming gold, running here and there.

The waves of grief that rock my soul, and threaten to engulf me,
Are also touched by golden light, as the sun rises to enfold me.

And that is how my life has been, a tapestry of light,
With little spots of darkness, to make the good times bright.

So as I weave the days ahead, my future 'days gone by',
I'd better make them beautiful, until my turn to die.

So all the ones I leave behind, their hearts so full of pain,
Will hold those golden threads, till the sun is shining again.

Finding the Way Back

White Sail

Shaft of light
Streaming from
Bruised clouds
Picks out
A solitary sail

Lifts it from
Something ordinary
To a sliver
Of purity
Adrift on a grey sea

Earthly Silk

Grasses, reeds
Swishing softly
Bending before the wind
Single emerald strokes
Of brilliance

The earth like a swathe of silk
Grasped by unseen hands
Lifted, draped
Like sheets on a bed
Billowing, settling

Shimmering with every breeze
Hillsides rippling
Mobile, fluid
Changing with each moment
Never still

Symphony of movement
Earthbound flight
Seed heads rattling
Whispering, sighing
Percussion in nature's orchestra

Grapes

Soft crack as green grapes
Explode in my mouth
Releasing echoes
Of summer heat
Dusty warm evenings

Row upon straight row
Vines marshalled along a wire
Uniformity that does not
Reach each grape
Whose flavour is fractionally different

Crisp skin
Firm flesh
Tantalising blend
Sensations as diverse
As dappled sunlight

Shimmering Diamond

Solitary drop of
Seawater
Dripped slowly
From my hair
Onto my arm

It lay there
Trembling
Like a shimmering
Diamond
Alive with inner fire

Cockatoos

Saturday morning
A chance to sleep in
Instead of awakening
To soft music
Temperate voices

Screeching raucous
Sulphur-crested cockatoos
Split the air
Feasting in the gum trees
Practising aerodynamics over the roof

Sending other birds
Into a frenzy
Of alarm calls
The sweet carolling
Of a magpie

Brings some semblance of order
Finches and sparrows
Call to each other daintily
Down in the riverbed
The cockatoos are still shouting

Liquid Glass

Mornings cloud evaporates beneath the sun
Waves break ceaselessly on the shore
Water, warm, surging and receding
Rocking motion to ease the soul
A smile eventually comes

Wind on the waters surface
Causes it to ripple in tiny movement
Shards of sunlight like broken mirrors
Reflect brilliantly
Flashing and dancing

Rollers break in a flurry of white
Opalescent colours in the heart of each wave
Around my legs, soft pressure
Green, clear, solid looking
Moving like liquid glass

Enchanted

A cool autumn breeze blew along the foreshore
I sheltered in the hollow of the sand dunes
To watch the brilliant golden orb
Sinking lower and lower, leaving a trail of gold light
That kissed each ripple with inner fire

Dusky pink and apricot, the sky was vibrant
With the flamboyant afterglow
More stunning than the actual setting of the sun
I turned to see the full moon had risen
Softly reflecting the fire of the now hidden sun

Hours later, unable to sleep
I walked along the deserted beach
The pristine moon shone off white sands
Each water-filled, small, gleaming curve
Held the image of a full moon

Hundreds of pale shells
Lay like upturned fairy cups
Cradling a full moon in their hearts
Adding to the enchantment
Of being surrounded by a sea of moons

Early the next morning
I walked out onto the jetty
Where last night the sun had set
The fragile tissue of the moon
Hung suspended over a bank of frail pink cloud

The path of light across the water
Was pure silver
The moon turned to pearly pink
As it slipped gracefully
Behind blue clouds

Over the hills
The clouds were shining vivid pink
Softening the grey water
Making it appear
Less cold and forbidding

Pink turned to gold
As the sun brightened the sky
Suddenly it was there
Blinding. Overpowering
Bringing life to the dawn stillness

Tranquillity

Soft tap
Sending petals
Falling
To lay on the floor
Their splendour spent

Dusty red
Like old velvet
Once luxuriant
Now faded
Still fragrant

Evoking an eternity
Of memories
Symbols of another
Language
Beyond words

Transcending
Geographical borders
Or barriers in a troubled mind
Bringing tranquillity
To the heart

Dawning

Dark velvet night
Star-studded skies
Distant moon casting eerie shadows
Keeping ignorant
Protected innocents

Awakening a silent stillness
A brightening that
Expands steadily
Revealed untold wealth
Nature's abundant beauty

Awe-filled obeisant
Unblinking eyes watch
The heraldic sun rise
Like a god's eye
From soft lemon clouds

Shimmering white-gold orb
Mesmerising spellbinding
Making diamonds of raindrops
Etching a pathway of light
Across a surging river

Fragment In Time

On an autumn afternoon
Tall trees reach
Tired arms overhead
To make a tunnel
Of the narrow street

Regal parade
Still, timeless
Silent sentinels
Guard of honour
Casting deep shadows

Eyes drawn irresistibly
Along a pathway
Of soft dappled light
To an archway
Of blazing purity

White silver gold
Dazzling shimmering
Breathtaking spellbinding
Beckoning 'come hither'
With all the enticement of a lover

Uncontained Joy

He wandered with no apparent purpose
Big floppy-brimmed hat to protect him
From the 108-degree heat forecast for today
He had that loose-limbed quality
Of the intellectually disadvantaged

Suddenly, he roared out 'Hey'
He stumbled in his haste
Arms reaching wide in welcoming embrace
Then clasping his hands in childlike glee
His joy was impossible to express

I looked up to see the subject of his attention
She walked towards him carefully
Small smile lighting up her shy features
Her greeting was more subdued but I could tell her heart
Was as warm as the colour of her pink shirt

Defiance

Close-cropped blonde hair
On a head held high
Her face was a turmoil
Of pensive defiance and misery
Daring anyone to pity her

With painstaking care
She crossed the road
Amid the midday traffic
Willing the lights not to change
Before she reached comparative safety

The empty leg of her trousers
Proclaimed the inevitability
Of her shiny new crutches
Growing in familiarity
Then becoming the missing limb

At the End of the Day

No one appeared to notice
The tragic plight
Of the elderly lady
Shuffling so slowly
Along the pavement

Dressed in a floral frock
Sun hat perched
On her grey hair
Cream shoes overwhelmed
By her swollen ankles

Her back was bent over
Pushing her face straight down towards the earth
A walking stick preventing her
From toppling over completely
However does she see the sun?

Parading Down the Parade

Like a regal goddess
She paraded down the Parade
We all watched her
Eyes drawn to her unusual long, blonde hair
And short, black dress

There was a straight line to her shoulders
That flowed down her back
Then flared over her hips
So with each step her skirt swung out
Emphasising her bare, tanned legs

Old men turned, yearning for lost youth
Women became self-conscious
Of sensible shoes, serviceable dresses
Children at their heels
All momentarily wanting to be someone else

Cheeky

As I took my customary stroll
Along the river path to the bus stop
The sun was already hot at seven in the morning
My usual reverie was interrupted
By the soft tinkle of a bicycle bell

Hastily stepping to the side
I only glanced at the cyclist
Who sped past, crouched low over his racer
Not for him careful protection from the sun
He wore only a 'G' string, helmet and sneakers

His long slim back was beautifully tanned
And gleaming with perspiration
His cheeks sported the same 'all over' tan
Each one cleverly tattooed
With what looked, at too brief a view, like a rose

Paradise Interchange

She was a tiny woman with white woolly hair
A cheap perm all her pension would stretch to
Frock of indiscriminate greens and blues
Her baggy cardigan the colour of much rain-washed old string
And glasses with old-fashioned thick, dark rims

She walked with a great sense of purpose
To the bus stop at the Paradise interchange
Handbag hooked securely over her arm
In the style of the Queen Mother
As if she were a proud, but poor relation

Clasped in her hand a magnificent bouquet of
Freshly cut frangipani flowers from her garden
Protected by plain, brown wrapping paper
The Paradise interchange took on new meaning
A parody of an exotic tropical island

Annette

No one gets to know an obedient child
Or hears about the dreams she had
While tidying her room and doing her homework
Caught between more forceful siblings
Who heard the too-quiet voice saying 'What about me?'

Just once, I saw the whole person
And the picture is permanently in my mind
So when I see and hear her struggling
To find her own place in the world
I have faith in that moment's revelation

She sat alone on a bench
On the far side of an island
Gazing out to an empty sea
Like a patient schoolgirl, or timeless woman
Totally at peace with herself

A Lament

Ah! What we could have had
If you had stepped outside your boundaries
I'm not condemning you for holding back
I wonder if you think of us
And miss the opportunity we had

We had so much to give each other
Perhaps we were both a little too afraid
I wanted to take you beyond
The person you portrayed to the world
To being at ease with the one inside

I could have shown you how to love yourself
We could have shared our love
Of music, the arts, literature
Instead, you chose to stay
A wistful bird in a gilded cage

Music In the Park

Late afternoon, in the heart of the city
The parklands lay dozing
Under an autumn sun
The air was fresh and still warm
The earth richly damp from long-awaited rain

The trees were dull green
With the tired look they wear
Just before cold nights
Turn them to a blaze of
Orange and yellow fire

The sky was clear blue and dotted
With picture-book puffy clouds
Sitting alone, cross legged on the grassy bank
A young man played his violin
There was no one close enough to hear except the ducks

Hard Road

Unless You Are Brave

Don't walk with me
Unless you are brave
Ready to test
Challenge
Old comfortable norms

I will not play
A nicer game
To ease your mind
I will make you
Question yourself

Thoughts feelings
Held down
Controlled
Forbidden credence
Because they are different

Don't turn on me
If you don't like
What you find
I didn't make you
I just opened your eyes a little

Living and Knowing

Standing by
Helpless agonising
Watching knowledge
Filter into a
Disbelieving soul

Living and knowing
Worse than death
No clean finale
Just a ragged banner
Blown by the wind

Shredded carelessly
Relentlessly eroded
By sun and rain
Till the colours are gone
The fibre decimated

Dreaming In the Sand

Autumn brings coolness
In the early morning
There are few people about
Seagulls diving for breakfast
Are good company

The ocean rushing to shore
Seems to be in a hurry
Casting up countless shells
Different shapes and sizes
Broken crab pieces

Solitary white rose
Thrown into the water
Returns on the next wave
Not rejected
Left dreaming on the sand

Discovery

I sought my pack
Yet I had moved among them
All along
They had circled me
Patiently waiting

Keeping distant
Protective
Respectful
Absorbing the overflow
Buffering the shocks

At last as I
Have conquered fear
I can meet their eyes
Surprised and moved
By what I see there

Depths of emotion
Compassion
Pleasure
Such warm affection
Pride that I have made it

The victory is not just mine
Rather a triumph
For everyone who has despaired
An unspoken bond
Between those who have overcome

A banner of hope perhaps
For those struggling still
With the oppression
Of an ever diminishing
Comfort zone

Veterans

Our eyes met
I looked away
Caught by that open
Welcoming smile
I looked again

I recognised her
And wondered
What she had seen
In my face
Hers was so full of joy

She was different
More than extra weight
Greying hair
A quiet surety
'I have come through'

We stood on the causeway
Halfway between two land masses
Both walking alone
Self-appointed therapy
To heal the sorrows of our lives

Our histories similar
Married young, offspring
Trying to please our husbands
Both being battered and beaten
Yet unquashed

Tragedy striking us
Through our children
Now strong enough
To take back our lives
To go on creatively

Like battle-scarred veterans
Our wars made us weak yet stronger
Now we spar with the memories
Walk alone
And write poetry

The Eleventh Hour

I sat at the Cenotaph
The city was awakening
Row upon row of little white crosses
Marched across the grass
Like the servicemen they represented

Where are the crosses for the rest?
The mothers, wives, sweethearts
Still waiting, over fifty years later,
For their man to come home
Still not believing he is dead

Why did anyone ever think
Glorifying the dead
Made them less so?
Honour them? Yes
For what life is worthy of less?

Grief has built a barrier
Between one reality and another
Time has dulled the pain
I function well most days
Even with joy and laughter

Where are you tears and brokenness?
At least in you there is relief
Better than this walled-off safety
That traps me in a kind of limbo
Where everything is muted and subdued

Let me sink below the surface
Or fly so high no one else can reach
And my thoughts can drift where they may
And I will not fear them
Or weary of their constancy

Laughter

My spirit felt cheerless
Wishing it were evening.
Stretching before me a day
The eastern sky
Brightened regardless

Grey clouds trembled
On the horizon
White gold almost violently
Poured out fingers of light
The sun split in two

The ocean lay dull
Green waves rolled onto the shore
Gradually soothed my mind
Sun broke through
Whitecaps shone

Shed shoes and stockings like weights
Danced barefoot at water's edge
Tiny waves sparkled with sunlight
Arms opened wide rejoicing
A heart overflowing with gladness

Childlike senses rushing
Fleeing cares, the caring
Music raising awareness
Freedom flooding the mind
Laughter bubbles unbidden

Long silent prayer of thanksgiving
Hugs the joy close
Too precious this gift to share
Feels the glow like a flame
Too long dimmed

Snowy gull sat on the sand
A black petrel flew overhead
Over the water a heron glided
Peace soaked my being
Lasting all day

Taming the Wild

I think of you my friend
Waiting patiently as I balance
The see-saw of emotions
You laugh with me
Would hold me if I could weep

Wisely you withhold your views
When you know, at that moment,
They will not serve the purpose
For which they were intended
Assessing carefully the right time to speak

My emotional instability frightens and frustrates me
I counsel my fears
Reminding myself they are not without foundation
I am not very good
At just drifting along

Your eyes are becoming more amber-coloured
I am still wary of looking into you
With you I feel like a wild animal
In need of comfort and nutrition
But untrusting of your humanness

A paradox with your lion eyes
How can it be, that you will tame me
Or will you set me free
Within the safe confines
Of your caring

Restoration

Sometimes, what I crave for more than anything else
Is solitude and silence.
Silence free of voices, even gentle ones
Wanting a response my tired mind
Does not wish to formulate

Silence free of music that pulls and tugs my senses
Like the branches of a weeping willow
Caught in a swirl of water
Silence free of the incessant rushing tide
Breaking on the shore, soothing, calming

Silence unbroken by the quiet chirp
Of an unseen, unknown bird
Settling to sleep in the dunes.
In my motel room I see my face in the mirror
Changing from old, to young and back again

As painful thoughts cross my mind
Always dark rings under my eyes give me away
Lines around my upper lip, where long term
Compression keeps me from screaming
Crying out against injustice and intolerance, stupidity and cruelty.

Now even the heavens weep as rain falls
I tuck chilled hands into my sleeves
Lay my head down on my arms and weep.
Water dripping somewhere outside
Sounds like someone tapping on the window

Do I want the attentions of a lover
Who would make me laugh
Make my senses and my mind
Fire up with lust and affection?
Just the thought has me smiling

Shaking my head at my own weakness
I gently admonish
'Don't let the bastards get you down,
Not even the lovely ones.
Reach for golden memories, fling them high and wide

Lift your face to see them dance
Fluttering softly, beautiful, beautiful moments of joy
Warm your hands and heart on their shining
Never mind that the mirror is not as kind as it used to be
There are still treasures in your soul waiting to be released.'

Watery Mind

Clear water
Moving constantly
Like thoughts
Never ceasing
Their ebb and flow

Carrying the
Flotsam and jetsam
Revealing hidden
Depths secrets
As yet unshared

Hoping for a pause
Respite time-out
The next step
Already plotted
By an unseen navigator

A deity
An ancient mariner
Another self
Needing to emerge
And fly free in the sun

Philosophising
To make acceptable
The peculiarities
Of the human mind
Searching for understanding

Grieve No More

Grieving mother
Let me go
I need to fly
Don't hold me
Down here

Feet shackled
To the floor
By your demands
I loved him
He was of me

Let me love him
My way
Not conventionally
But freely
Openly

Let me love him now
As I couldn't
When he was alive
I don't want him
To be dead

Sunday-afternoon Amazon

Amid Sunday-afternoon prudery
She strode
Amazon-like
Out of the water
Across the sands

Short sturdy body
Full breasts
Wide hips
Springing to life
With a lover's touch

Four times
She has known
The labour
Of bringing forth
New life

Sons that tested
Courage fortitude
Forging a spirit
Even death
Could not break

Now, aloof serene
Half smiling
Exulting in separateness
Warmed by the sun's kiss
Caressed by a sea breeze

Dreams

In our quiet centre
Dreams aspire
Hopes bask
In sunshine
And slowly flourish

Dreams as different
As each dreamer
All precious
As life itself
None less important

For some
Ambitious complex
Building empires
Taking over other lives
Ignoring the cost

For others
A simple desire
To make people feel good
With a word
Or a gentle touch

Seduction

Sun's rays, warm
For a winter's day
Ocean inviting
Ever seductive voice
Calling 'Come hither'

'Come play
In my cold embrace
I will invigorate your skin
Make your soul gasp
In unexpected pleasure'

And the promise was fulfilled
You took my breath away
Made me aware of my body
Luxuriating in the surging tide
As liberating as passions release

Stirring Passions

Enchanted morning
Warm, soft sand
Fresh wind
Whipping waves
Spray feathering

Clothes flapping
Laughter springs
Bubbling like the foam
Senses soar
Riding lofty thermals

Freemans Cove
Yachts tied to their moorings
Bobbing, tugging
Trying to free themselves
To run with the tide

Fly unfettered
Before the wind
Skimming the ocean swells
Exultant exhilarated
Blissfully aware

Lovers touch
Stirring passions
Till body and soul
Melt with liquid fire
Consuming healing

Dying Brightness

There in an air of suspended movement
More than the sun setting
The evening is closing in all around
There will be a cold night
And the air is already misting

All sounds grow muffled
The gulls not so raucous
The skimming willy-wagtails falter
A faint haze appears from nowhere
We collectively hold our breath

At this moment of absolute sacredness
A passing seagull's wings
Are turned to pure gold
The tiny sliver of the moon
Gathers the suns dying brightness to itself

If I no long had any sight
This golden brilliance
Would be a wonderful final vision
To be softly remembered
Like loved ones' faces

Innocence

Sleeping child
Hand open trustingly on the pillow
Eyelashes lying curved
Upon rosy cheeks
Dimpled with inner mirth

Little mouth
Half smiling
Knowing already
The sensuousness
Of suckling a breast

Sturdy legs
One day will travel far
To satisfy a curious mind
Row of tiny toes
To balance each step

Tiny hands
Like starfish
Patting fairies
Flitting over the cradle
Watching the infant

Pudgy feet
Kicking juggling
Transparent bubbles
Toes wriggling
When they burst

Unfocused eyes
Pools of mystery
Ever watchful
Absorbing everything
Unconditionally

Sticky Little Hands

Long, long waves
Reaching forever
Rising high, gathering sunlight
Overturning on a wisp of white
Then crashing thunderously on the shore

Soft, sticky little hand thrust trustingly in mine
Dragging us toward the tumbling foam
Then screeching in mock terror
As we fled the oncoming water
Only to turn and do it over again

We laughed at spaghetti seaweed
Bogged cars in the sand
And ate ice cream
Fitting behaviour for this grandmother
With my eldest grandchild

Delighting in memories when my sons were young
And they had sticky little hands
Filled with priceless treasures
A furry caterpillar, wild flowers
Roses from a neighbours garden

Presented to me
With all the pomp and ceremony befitting royalty
Yet I was the humbled one, my joy to serve
Service that lasted years
A lifetime of listening, holding back the impulse

To hold them in my arms
Protecting them too much
Not the same this new generation
Mine all the pleasure, his parents' responsibility
Guiding these sticky little hands

Published

I raced home from work
Impatient with speed restrictions
At last the postie
Had brought the book
With my poem on the first page

I bubbled over with excitement
Wanted to sing and laugh out loud
Shout to everyone as I went by
'My poem has been published
Look at me. I did it

And just you wait
One day I will have
An entire book published
All of my own work
Then hear my acclamation.'

Those In the Sea

On a pretty autumn day I drove to the Coorong
Walked across the soft sand of the dunes.
I stood alone on an empty beach
Looking south west and thinking
There is only sea till the ice of the Antarctic

As the great rollers thundered in
I turned to face north and watched
The mirrored sun, white on the water
I turned to face south and watched
The sea mist obscure the sands

My thoughts went to those
Who populate the oceans
Whale, seal and dolphin
All held as symbols of life, living in peace and harmony
At home in the symbol of emotions

I thought of the whales
Singing their songs
Echoing for countless fathoms
Enormous bodies housing even bigger hearts
Holding knowledge we can only dream of, strive for

I thought of the seals
Source of many folk tales
Of being turned into maidens
And returning again to the sea
Deep dark sorrowful eyes forever weeping

I thought of the dolphins
Culmination of fluid motion
Racing ships, surfing waves
Leaping flashes of silver
Bringing us only joy

Pause For a Moment

Upstream from the weir, the river paused, and gathered strength
To take it rushing down toward the sea
Here it lay in pristine stillness
Reflecting an early morning sky in minute detail
Not a flicker, a ripple, marred the mirror-like surface

Soft, so soft, the whisper of a breeze
Began to dispel the oppressive heat
That had weighted the gaiety of life.
Hair lifts from hot faces
Allowing rosy-apple cheeks to cool

On an old decaying wooden garden fence
A rambling rose lodged in peaceful somnambulance
Its blooms nodding, delicately pink
Filling the air with fragrance
Calming senses to match the stillness of the water

Evening

The distant hills are blanketed in cloud
The sounds of evening whisper their being
Water is dripping from the overflow pipe
And rattling down the path
To the thirsting garden

The gum tree stands with leaves drooping
Dust washed away, leaving them a paler green
A row of raindrops hang like beads
From the balcony railing and branches alike
A tiny moth dances with death

The fishpond is lapping its rocky edges
The surface trembling with odd raindrops
The father magpie is cracking seeds on the porch
He is wet and bedraggled
With head feathers spiked like a rebellious teenager

Mother and baby have zoomed into the garden
The three of them are having a conversation in the tree
They too have come down for supper
Their voices are soft and gentle
Not like the other bird-alarm calls I can hear down by the river

The potted geranium is sending out
A sweet, refreshing perfume now it is wet
The house is still hot and clammy
No doubt the mosquitoes will be out soon
I will relinquish my position – graciously

Smoke Gets In Your Eyes

I burned the toast again.
I tossed it out onto the midnight garden
And it glowed red as a tiny breeze caught it
It was then I saw how bright the moon was
I stopped to pray, 'Please don't let me get lost'

When I came back indoors
The kitchen was hazy with smoke
I flicked the switch for the ceiling fan
And watched in fascination as the drifting tendrils
Were sucked steadily upward

Like the second cup of tea
Is never as good as the first
My second piece of toast
Uniformly browned – not even a little burned
Was missing something – that which filled the air

A Moment of Grace

Whilst making a last cup of tea before going to bed
I felt warmth and silence surround me
The walls of my little house would protect me from the
	outside world
Within myself, I felt the quiet surety
That can only come from being loved and respected

The night before, I babysat two of my grandsons
Daniel consulted the street directory and discovered
The roads on the map don't always match the ones the car
	travelled along
He kept me entertained with the same matter-of-fact logic
His father has amazed me with for thirty years

Kyle, much younger, treated me with studied indifference all
	evening
Yet, when on the verge of slumber, I put him in his cot
I felt something flow between us – impossible to describe
Our eyes met briefly, then, with total trust, he turned over
	and went to sleep
That moment of grace is forever a part of me

Home To the Sun

My eyes are dazzled by the sun
Reflected in a blinding path
Over the ocean from shore to horizon
Dozens of seagulls have gathered
Bathing in the brightness

A lone yacht heads for home
Single sail dark against the sky
Will it be drawn up by the sun
Disappearing forever in the blaze
Or navigate safely to the waiting harbour

Will the sun forgive the idiocy of mankind
And return tomorrow
Giving us another chance
To forget our own selfish greedy needs
And do it right for the planet?

Lovely Surprise

While I sat oblivious, at the table
Eating my breakfast, reading a book
The sky outside had begun to brighten
The first soft bird calls
Were spreading the news

A voice on the radio
Broke through my concentration
To tell me it was time
To continue the preparations needed
To set off for work for another day

I went to the sink with my dishes
And my breath was taken away in wonder
By the sight of glowing, bright pink clouds
Hanging like curtains over the hills
Reminding me the weatherman had forecast rain

Some little while later I left the house
The sky now was clear and pale
Those clouds had thinned to almost nothing
High overhead a tiny, waning sickle moon
Shone with a green light

Debarking

Day after long day, summer passed
The heat so stifling it denied the movement
Yet those days could be ticked off on the calendar
Who cared for statisticians who cheerily claimed
The longest spell over 35 in recorded history?

Trees, young and lissome, or giant and patient gums
Their skin drying out and cracking
At night great shards rustling to the ground
Sharp sounds, hard and loud
Like the texture of the fallen bark

A strong wind blasted through
Stripping mercilessly, bark and leaves alike
Then the rain, singular, splatting drops
Gathering momentum, to a torrential downpour
The noise of them on the roof obliterating everything else

Rivers of water running down the tree trunks
Seeking to slide between new tender skin
And the dried out scabs of last season
Curls of russet and ochre
Rolling over with the strain

A final gust of wind releasing their desperate hold
Letting them fall to the sodden earth
And becoming entangled in lower branches
Or to cluster among brave new foliage
Drying out, waiting for the next storm

Icelandic Poppies

I didn't realise when I saw them
Huddled, in tightly bound bunches of buds
That they would be so incredibly lovely
When the warmth of the office
So quickly coaxed them open

Their colours are so bright and pure
Different hues, from deep orange
Reaching to the palest yellow
Their petals are tissue thin
With a slightly crumpled look of the newborn

They are so fresh and vibrant
With a cutting clarity reminiscent of
Pristine snowfields
Unsullied by industrial waste
And the unmistakable footprint of man

I had visions of acres and acres of them
Under an ice-blue sky
Perfume carried on a sharp breeze
However does such delicacy
Withstand the restless winds?

Homeward Bound

Pilgrimage

Silent, inexorable
Golden fingers of dawn
Reach across the heavens
Banishing night's terrors
As mist evaporates in sunlight

A solitary figure stands
Arms outstretched, in supplication
Eyes, tear-filled, beseeching
A merciful deity for courage
To walk another day with joy

A running tide
Sounds like the hurrying footsteps
Of beloved friends and family
Bestowing the most precious gift
Unconditional love, unquestioning acceptance

Sleepy birds croon the day to a close
A full moon rides high
Shrouded in diaphanous cloud
Distant thunder rumbles a warning
The weary pilgrim pauses

Tapestry of Sound

Strings blend harmonies
That take the spirit
In a flight
Soaring sweeping
Carelessly cascading

Drifting feather-like
Caught momentarily suspended
To roll like thunder
Richocheting around the mountain tops
Reverberating in deep caverns

Plucking melodies
From the wind
Whispering, haunting
Weaving a tapestry of sound
With rainbow threads

Then airy as mist
Disappearing into nothing
Leaving only an echo
Gathering in the ether
To pour again

Go To Hell

My safe earth trembled and quaked beneath my feet
Each step I took landed on unstable ground
I cried out in anguish, thinking some unseen hand
Was taking over my life, pulling strings
Making me dance, when I wanted to be still

I thought I was comfortable in my self-made world
Accepting times of despair as fellow travellers
Almost welcoming the times when I just wanted
To curl up, go to sleep and never wake up
Secretly hoping each time, I would have the courage to go.

Ah, guilt! You fucking insidious monster!
You perched on my shoulder and almost ground me down.
I let you stay there. I gave you house room.
You almost demolished my good memories
Then made me feel worse for wanting you gone.

There was no unseen hand causing this breakthrough.
It was myself, at last saying 'Enough'
I did the best I could.
I will do better for myself from now on.
Guilt, you can go to hell in a basket. I don't need you any more!

Gone Forever

My son, gone forever from my arms
Taking with you part of the sun
Leaving me a shadow
A tapestry of life woven of countless
Coloured threads, rich, vibrant, muted, subdued

Your memory gifting pure gold that nothing can tarnish
Illuminating bleak despair
Seated at your grave, I count the blessings
Your death becoming
A greater gift than your life

Stronger than grief will ever be
Now joyous freedom for both of us
Only you know what
You have been freed of
I can wonder and be glad for you

I have been freed of worrying about you
And left with wonderful memories
And loving you
You will be forever young, brave and beautiful
I will go on getting richer

It's All Right, Mark

I know you told me ten years ago
'It's all right, mum'
And your gift has held me safe
With some degree of sanity
Throughout the passing of time

As I struggled one morning
And found the words that simply stated
I don't want you to be dead
So this morning the words found me
'It's all right, Mark'

Grief has so many different faces
I have wept for you
I have wept for myself
Now I see I have been weeping
For us all

Silver Cord

The clatter of hobnailed boots on cobblestones
Announced my paternal grandfather's arrival
Home from his allotment, brandishing a bunch of turnips
With all the aplomb of a royal gardener
Exhibiting his prize-winning, exotic, hybrid roses.

My dad gifted my mother the bounty of the countryside
Posies of early bluebells and cowslips, a hat full of mushrooms
Baskets of apples and cherries to preserve
Armloads of logs for cheerful, winter fires
Swathes of berry-laden holly, ivy and mistletoe

Born midway through the century, I was blessed with a brave heart
Which took me to the other side of the world
Where my sons now walk, strong and tall
As children, presenting me with wild flowers, seashells and dreams
As adults, the sweetest gift of all – continuity

I watch, wonder-filled, my eldest grandson,
Poised in contemplation, his stance is like my dad's
I see my mother in the smile of the youngest child
The line reaches through each passing generation
Linking us forever, by a silver cord.

Afterword

I am no tall poppy, yet I have lived an extraordinary life. For as long as I can remember I was encouraged to 'make friends' and 'mix more socially'. I have no doubt these encouragements were well meant. I think it rather sad that so few people have recognised that I am not lonely in my own company. I freely admit there are times when the longing to be with one or other particular person, becomes an unbearable ache in my arms, but I don't confuse this with loneliness or being afraid to be with myself.

I have collected any number of philosophical gems over the years. I even used to write them down in a book. I loaned that little book to someone once, and, perhaps not realising its value to me, they didn't return it and it was thrown out with other out-dated belongings when they moved on. Regardless of this thoughtlessness, I have kept the golden yardsticks that I now choose to live my life by.

As a child growing up in a tiny English village, it was not stated, 'Be brave enough to be different.' I just was. I had two older brothers and wherever they went I tagged along. I climbed the same trees, searched for squirrels and birds nests just like them. It didn't occur to me I was supposed to do things differently because I was a girl. In fact, I remember being quite put out that I was not allowed to join the Boy Scouts. Girl Guides was for girls and I wasn't interested at all.

The advantage of a good education in an all-girls high school did nothing much to teach me about being socially acceptable. En masse I learned girls are most unkind if your hair wasn't curly in just the right way, or you wore a hand-knitted jumper instead of the fashionable one from Marks and Sparks. As for being a farmer's daughter, and proud of it, well, that put me right out on the edge.

This separateness drove me to the library, where I found a home from home. I discovered books and poetry that took me far from the peer-group pressure of average suburban minds, standards taught from generation to generation without thought.

Once freed of the expectations of school life, my instincts flourished. Opportunities presented themselves and if it felt right, I did it. Unconsciously I was getting in touch with my implicit faith that I will always have what is right for me, when it is right. Many a time I have fought and railed against the timing, but eventually with patience, and without exception, this faith has proven to be absolutely right for me.

I can hear gasps of 'irresponsible' or 'thoughtless'. Perhaps. However, there is not a person alive who will ever convince me it was wrong for me to marry an itinerant Irish barman. He took me to live in Ireland for a year. We emigrated to Australia with two babies under two years old and found a better life for all of us. We went on and had two more sons. How can anyone say it was wrong to have such beautiful children who have grown up to be wonderfully perceptive and sensitive men, who have inherited their parents disregard for the ordinary and conventional?

Like most people, I took much of my life for granted. I did, however, gradually see that I had stopped waking in the morning delighted with the gift of a new day to be filled with interesting things to be seen or done. My marriage was an example of two people with very different dreams and aspirations and neither was able to 'convert' the other and compromise did not appear to be in our vocabulary.

Now I can see we all carry life's scars. In those early years I was totally unprepared for the complexities of human nature. In fact, I have lived my entire life being bewildered by people.

My naivety was probably a blessing and a bane for my husband. He loved me. He dedicated his life to providing for and protecting us all, yet it was a terrible irony that this commitment blinded and deafened him to differing visions and ideas. A combination of overwork and alcohol took its toll. It seemed to me he wanted to know my ideas then systematically tried to destroy them and in turn my credibility. I became a battered wife. Not in the obvious sense of broken bones or blackened eyes. My mind, my emotions, my spirit were being desecrated and I knew I had to leave to save my life and my sanity.

I was alone in Australia. All my relatives were in England.

I shattered my family unit when I moved out, taking my youngest aged ten and the eldest aged twenty. About eighteen months later, while I was still in shock from making this move, and with no chance for any healing to have begun, the final vestiges of my world crumbled completely.

In the space of nine months, my youngest son went back to live with his father, my second son committed suicide, my third son went off to live with friends and my eldest married his childhood sweetheart. Essentially, I had lost all of my boys.

Mark's suicide was not just the end of his life, it represented to me vindication of every negative thing my husband had ever said about me. Long, long after the divorce, his voice can still reduce me to a shuddering heap.

So how does one rebuild a person?

My mother, bless her heart forever, gave me the cornerstone when I was only a child. 'Rise above it, darling, just rise above it.' Deceptively simple but I doubt if truer words have ever been spoken.

As part of the 'having what is right for me, when it is right', people and books have come and gone in and out of my life. I don't believe anyone comes my way by chance. Always there has been an exchange of thoughts, ideas and experiences, and, while few have physically stayed, the value of those exchanges has been priceless and kept me going through times of terrible despair and desolation.

After the first year of numbness, reality would not be ignored. Saving grace comes in many forms. Working for a government department, my job put me in direct contact time and again with people far worse off in every sense of the word than I will ever be. It was a great leveller for self-pity.

The people I worked with were a constant, mostly silent, almost tangible embrace of unquestioning belief in me that no matter how many times I stumbled and fell, I could, and would, keep getting back up to take another step, even if it was only to prove their belief in me was not misplaced.

One man saw something in me at thirty-five that I had thought died many years earlier. He made me feel eighteen again and quite capable of re-starting my life any way I wanted it to be. It saddens me that he never appeared to have known how deeply I cared for him or how I treasure his gift of 'seeing me'. I admire him tremendously for the hard work he does to effect much needed changes in our society. I hope that one day he will take the time to allow himself to be healed of his own life's scars.

Another was my friend through the dreadful time of fear and insecurity when I acknowledged I had to leave my marriage if I was to live. His constant cheerful support, belief in me and plain, practical help were beyond measure. He taught me too, the pleasure of physical closeness with another, the beautiful expression of affection in touching.

Another stayed with me after Mark died. His own health issues demanded he keep to a strict lifestyle. He made me eat meals when I didn't want to bother. He taught me by example that every day you get up, have a shower, have breakfast and 'do' the day. For him to give up doing this, literally, meant death. He encouraged me to survive.

I had other choices too. I needed to share my life with people of a joyous and self-respectful nature. I needed to feel the joy of living again.

Mark died in 1991. Annette has been with me since shortly after that event. So much I don't remember of those years frightens me. I must have broadened her mind more than she could possibly have really wanted over the years as she listened to the gradual outpourings of my soul. Annette says I broke her heart too, but added she wouldn't have had it any other way. Through my experiences she was also living every parent's nightmare of losing a child. Annette fathomed under the turmoil and helped me trust my own instincts. She nudged and shoved me along gently and still 'socks' it to me now and then when I need it. It was to her that I have turned so many times and said, 'I don't think I can do this any more. I just want to sleep and not wake up.' She never said, 'Yes, you can', but led me along till I could say, 'Yes, I can do this.' We have developed a phrase: 'sailing ships'. She hangs me on my own logic, beliefs and arguments every time and then sits back laughing, saying, 'Sailing ships.' We are like two children in a schoolyard. How can you possibly put a value tag on a friend like that?

After three or four years, the enormity of having to live the rest of my life carrying the grief and loss of my son, my marriage and all my dreams was too much. I went out to suicide. But at every bend on that mountain road, where I was going to drive off into oblivion, there was my most beloved friend's face, with his cheeky smile and sparkling blue eyes. I could not run him over. He is constancy personified. He has made climbing mountains fun, because no matter where I go, he is right there with me. Together, he, Annette and my children have stopped 'hope' being a dirty word for me.

The day after discovering I wasn't ready to die, my friend and I talked about this. He asked me if I had a dream of my own. I searched within and saw the only dream that was really mine was to be a published author. I jokingly referred to writing the 'great Australian novel' but fact is stranger than fiction and I knew writing from my own experiences was the only way for my words to be real. I started writing poetry.

I love poetry because I can use the minimum number of words for maximum effect. The first year it was observations of nature, finding something in every day that made it special. The second year, I dared myself to write about people. I watched people. I listened to them. I found too many were unaware of the wonderful gift of their life and the world about them. I looked inside myself to 'write out' the heartaches as if by sharing them with others they would not be so overwhelming. I watched, albeit from a distance, how my sons struggled to come to terms with the loss of their brother and their childhood family.

Through my writing, I wanted to make people stop and think.

I am a devotee of the public library. Since those schooldays, books have been my escape and my comfort. When all else failed, I could always get lost in a book. Historical novels are a great way of learning about people and different cultures. I select volumes, take them home and begin to read and think, 'What on earth am I doing with this thing?' yet cannot put it down. By persevering, I find a few words among the many that give me a perfect understanding of an unrest in my mind.

Someone suggested I enter a poem in a competition. I didn't win but my poem was published in an anthology. For all my love of words, there simply aren't any that can describe the feeling of achievement.

I wanted to have a book of my own poems published because now I can look over my shoulder in amazement and wonder at where I have been, who I have shared my life with, just how wonderful the gift of life is, especially when you take a good hard look at it and the unlimited opportunities for growth.

I will always have four sons. However, such was the devastation when Mark died, I pushed my other sons to a safer distance. It was nothing to do with how much I loved them, how I hungered to see them or hear their voices. It was pure, undiluted fear that every time I saw them, this might be the last time. I cannot describe the agony of that terror and I denied us all the benefit of much needed comfort and healing. I still have terrible difficulty when we have a gathering as, for me, there is always one missing from the table.

I have no idea what I did, in this lifetime or a previous one, that my sons are so constant to me. The depths of their respect and caring are only really now becoming known to me. I have long admired their staggering loyalty to their father. They have shown courage and integrity as each has found a partner of strength and character. They have gifted me thus far with four grandsons. They have filled me with hope and joy for the future of the world with people like them in it.

I have had an extraordinary life, but it took the death of my son to make me see it. The price will always be too high.

Everyone has a story. It would be foolish indeed to make

comparisons, for there is always someone better or worse off than oneself. However, there is a comforting and healing sense of kinship with others who have had similar experiences.

Even death, that which we call the last act of our play, does not end a story. Everyone who has existed, no matter how briefly, affects someone else for the rest of their life. They affect others and so the story goes on and on. Perhaps, when grief and heartache isolates us, we forget this.

We cannot always control what touches our lives. We do all have the gift of choice. We can choose how we are going to allow ourselves to be affected. Bitterness seeps in unnoticed if we are not vigilant and sours everything we do, think and say.

There is much to be learned from watching how Mother Nature heals the wounds inflicted by uncaring, thoughtless mankind. By watching others, we can use them as an example of how we do, or don't, want to be. The choice is ours. Even no decision is a decision.

Whether we like it or not, we are all, ultimately, responsible for ourselves. It is not such a bad thing to visualise the kind of person we want to be and work towards that. I believe implicitly, by doing this, what is right for me will always come, when it is right for me…

www.ingramcontent.com/pod-product-compliance
Lightning Source LLC
Chambersburg PA
CBHW062145100526
44589CB00014B/1692